Still Standing

Rebecca English

Presentation by *BookLeaf Publishing*

Web: www.bookleafpub.com

E-mail: info@bookleafpub.com

ISBN: 9789358733945

First edition 2023

DEDICATION

"Still Standing" is lovingly dedicated to my mom, the late Margaret Beaufort, my daughter Emerald, my son Noel, and my grandson Amir. My mom has always been my cheerleader and a mighty Woman of God. She always taught me that when she left this world Jesus would never leave me nor forsake me. She was a strong woman and a role model in my life. My children encourage me to keep being who God made me to be.

"My grace is sufficient for you, for my power is made perfect in weakness." Therefore, I will boast all the more gladly about my weaknesses, so that Christ's power may rest on me." (II Corinthians 12:9)

Thank you for believing in me!

ACKNOWLEDGEMENT

I would like to express my special thanks and gratitude to God who is the sustainer of my life and the lifter of my head (Psalm 3:3). To my parents, the late Johnny and Margaret Beaufort, and my siblings who have transitioned Amanda, Earvin, Merrick and Costella, my siblings who still encourage me today, Johnny, Jr., Frank, Carol, Helen, Cynthia, Berthinia, Rendella, George, friends, and all of the people who have helped me become the person I am.

To my mom who taught me that Jesus would always be there in the time of trouble.

To my oldest sister Carol, who fights Sickle Cell Anemia every day, yet she encourages me daily to keep living.

To my siblings who taught me that family means everything and when everything else fails, family will always be there.

To my daughter, Emerald, who taught me that love is unconditional and I have a lot to share, and who taught me that she enjoys seeing how I am a blessing to others.

To my son, Noel, who taught me through his jokes that laughter is good for the soul.

To my grandson, Amir who lets me know through his hugs and kisses that I am the best Nana in the whole-wide-world.

To my nieces and nephews who allow me to be me and who view me as a survivor and prayer warrior.

To my friends who taught me that true friendship is rare and priceless.

To my Pastor, Elder Trevon D. McClary, Founder of Freedom Worship Center, thank you for encouraging me through your rich sermons.

A special thank you to my editors, my niece Jennifer H., my sister Carol S., my niece Elesha C., my daughter Emerald H., my son Noel E., and my best friends Charlise H. and Wanda H.

Thank you to everyone I acknowledged for helping me become the woman I am. "Still Standing" would not be in existence today without my testimonies and the relationships that resulted because of my encounters with you all on this journey.

PREFACE

In "Still Standing," I am in awe of how God has kept and blessed me. "Still Standing" allows me to utilize the advice I have often given to students I taught and encountered, "You can do whatever or be whoever you want to in life." My testimonies have taught me as I have encouraged acquaintances, friends, family members, and students who came across my path, that the sky's the limit, and "God is able to do exceedingly and abundantly above all we can ask or think according to the power that worketh in us." With God, nothing is impossible, all things are possible if you believe.

Life is a journey, and it reminds me of the popular adage, "Nobody said that the road would be easy!" As my mom used to sing, "I don't believe He brought me this far to leave me." II Corinthians 4:8-9 says, "We are troubled on every side, yet not distressed; we are perplexed, but not in despair; persecuted, but not forsaken; cast down, but not destroyed." In life, we may become shattered but with God's grace, He can heal the broken and put us back together again.

Handling life's circumstances can be exhausting. Looking to the Higher Power will definitely change our perspective and how we handle situations in life. How much are we willing to surrender? Partially surrendering won't do! Total surrender is the key.

Still Standing

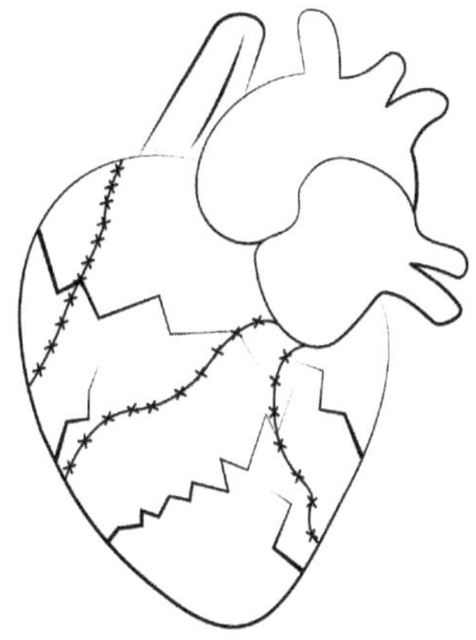

Broken, Broken
Over, Again
I thought I was going to die
Then I whispered, "Lord, why?"

God's breaking me
Like branches on a tree
Breaking me out of my limitations
Still standing, He's preparing unique
manifestations

Brokenness of the soul, I try to hide
Signs of brokenness locked up inside
Life's situations like a butterfly's metamorphosis
changes
Still standing, but no longer broken, He adjusts
and rearranges

Fragmented pieces, broken was I without
borders
Shattered pieces exist no more, passing through
deep waters
God's now my lifeline past, present, future, and
forever
I'm still standing, He whispered, "It was My
pleasure"

Stand up, I heard God cheerfully state
Now healed and set free, no more heavyweights
So glad I'm still standing, have a hunger and
longing for the Lord
Solving my own problems no longer can I afford

Reality convincing, staring me dead in my face
I recognized He saved me from death with His
loving grace
No more brokenness, I am renewed, refreshed,
and brand new
Ready to live again, the spirit of brokenness I
outgrew

The Importance of Dry Seasons

In the middle of seasons facing droughts
Back against walls, no strong force could bring me out

Seasons when nothing appeared to go right
Breathing still, suffocating air stiff tight

Everywhere I gazed, no sign of rain
On mountains' tops in valleys low, no gain

Growing and stretched, yet I go no further
Hurting in pain, Lord, I need you to nurture

Thoughts outgrew me, stifled vibrant dreams
Unfulfilled, fiery cravings haunting me it seems

My mind in the right posture, Comforter to be found
Never-ending droughts, still standing on firm ground

Blurred vision, dulling my ability to see
Drought's destination clear, saving me from me

Stretching

Embracing life's journey, pursuit is stirring
Brusquely realizes nothing is involuntarily
working

Paradigms, blurry visions, dreams to my surprise
All unclear and stagnant camouflaged in
disguise

Instantaneously out of nowhere, strength arises
in my face
Eagerly unlatching from that poignant, piteous
place

Restored strength, full of God's fresh mercy

Being stretched with new unwanted controversy

Visions began to precede me, conundrum at
work
Being stretched disorientation stubbornly will
still lurk

Be patient, His approved diagnosis is clear
Outgrowing where I am as He speaks is what I
hear

Momentum and mobilization, no longer out of
reach for me
Adhering to His voice now being stretched
willfully

The Power In This Hour

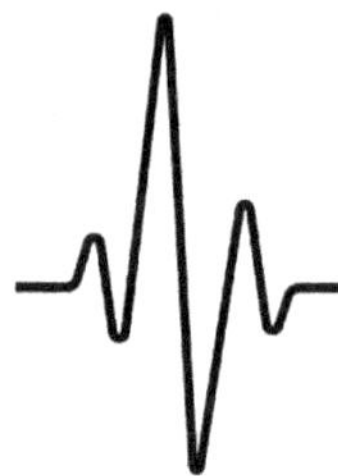

I've always wanted to be used by God in this
hour
I did my best, grew to acknowledge, it is He
who gives us Power

It's appealing to be the very best I can
Without Jesus' Spirit and Power, I'm just man

The one You created on that miraculous day in
the garden

Till sin showed up through satan never begging
for pardon

If the devil knew God's plan for man was to give
redemption
In his conversation with Eve, he would not have
used deception

Now that he fell into God's redeeming trap
Salvation and the cross fell at man's feet and in
his lap

Giving man an open opportunity to be with God
forever
Losing his place in heaven, beguiling Eve, I
know satan wished he'd never

All to give man the chance to receive His Holy
Spirit with Power
To perform miracles, signs, and wonders in this
very hour

Now's the day and time to utilize the gifts of the
Fivefold
Witness His extraordinary Power, unveil the
truth, and let it be told

It's His Supernatural Power that makes us whole
Yield to Jesus immediately, don't lose your soul

The Master Teacher

Took on a whole lot that I thought I could handle
Could do nothing without the passing of His
mantle
Those unwanted thoughts popped into my head
No longer my will but His will instead

Serving the Master from then till now
Learning has become my inevitable friend, I see
how
Lessons He designed, others I chose
It's the morals I had to learn to decisively
transpose

Experiences like fire nearly extinguished me
Master Teacher transforms my mind and sets it
free
Somehow my human nature began to fight back
New levels arose, and old levels attacked

The Master Teacher is omnipotent, He'll disclose
My mistakes demonstrated His Power to expose
Revealing His Power is definitely a must
Yielding to the Master is His purpose for us

The Danger of Poison

Once I thought poison came only from a
venomous snake
Satan's not only in a serpent's form, make no
mistake
Until I encountered it on a Sunday, too late

Lurking in the church camouflaged using the
Word
Penetrated my mind, body, and soul, love
turning into hate absurd
Like a wildfire, it rapidly spread without delay,
unheard

Highly disappointed why should I convert
Realizing everyone is not saved in the church, it
hurt
The enemy lies and schemes, don't abort, Jesus
will assert

Poison causes fiery, darts and targets whoever
Give your life to Christ, He'll protect you
forever
He'll never leave or forsake you, no never

Using the excuse the Creator made me from dirt

Methods not based on scripture, caution alert
Broadcasting unholy forms of godliness in the
church, divert

Playing the victim like you've been dragged
through the mud
Don't listen to those voices, you're still loved
Jesus will forgive, for you, He bled and shed his
blood

Your Capacity

I gave my life to Christ
Brokenness competed with my life

My trials felt like 1,000 years
My pain was so crucial, I cried no tears

I made it through one issue after another
Only the Father knew that I could make it even
further

I felt the pain had reached my capacity
The answer I found was to dig deeper actually

Eyes have not seen, neither have ears heard
There's more to capacity, dig deeper into the
Word

As I dug deeper, at an angle from my eyes was
the devil
Tried to suppress my capacity to prevent my
next level

God knew how much my portion would contain
Watching myself drowning, I had to refrain from
drowning again

Understanding the pressure I thought I couldn't
endure
I'm still standing because it was the pressure that
blessed me even more

I'm Blessed

Sunshine or rainy days
Really doesn't matter cause I'll be okay
'Cause there's someone who really cares
No matter what my issues are He's always there

It's not always keeping joy inside
Life's not always fair but I'm still satisfied
I just keep it movin' and I wear a smile
'Cause I know He'll fix it in a little while

I'm blessed

Yes He favors me
He just keeps on blessing me, blessing me

So glad He's chosen me
To go and tell the world that salvation's free
I'm never on my own
I never have to face the enemy alone

I keep praising Him even when I'm in pain
There could be no sunny days without the rain
Standing on His promises you just can't lose
There's only one thing left to do and that is to
choose

I'm blessed
Yes He favors me
He just keeps on blessing me, blessing me

Anyway You're blessing me, blessing me
Anyway You're blessing me it's alright!

It Was Necessary

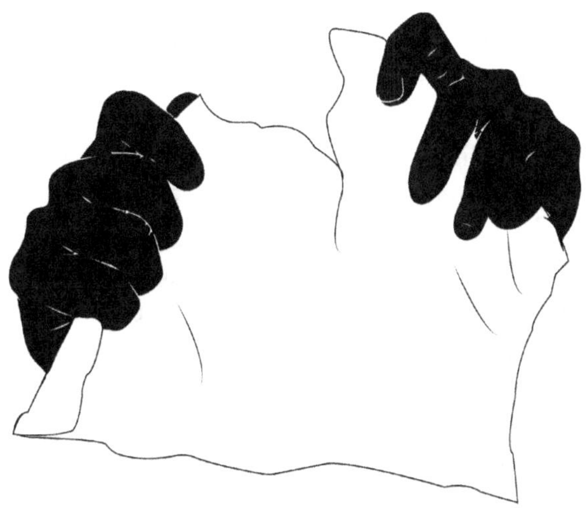

Live each day, life will happen
Life was more than I could imagine

I should have remembered the Word
Not to think it strange when life occurred
It was necessary

Don't just give me a Word to appease me
I lived to witness the road isn't easy

Over time, I learned to walk in God's authority
Winning battles became my priority
It was necessary

The Holy Ghost filled me with Power
Got no choice but to exercise it in this hour
Can no longer continue living and be defeated
The devil's game plan has been depleted
It was necessary

Functioning at new levels in this seasonal shift
To be victorious accept the gifts

That same day He died on the cross
The blood prevented me from being lost
It was necessary

It's up to me to declare what I bind and decree
Realizing Jesus had already provided everything
for me
It was incredibly necessary

The Potter's Wheel

Sat down at the Potter's wheel
Molding the clay marred in His hands He'll feel
The final outcome He wanted to reveal

Dreams crushed, shattered, and broken
In His hands, He formed another chosen
Temperature control brings out the emotion

Firm hands applied, pressure definitely a must
Sculpturing doesn't feel good but He'll adjust
Totally for God to get us to gain His trust

His Will while on that configuring wheel I
thought I knew
Unexpected paths were a part of His design too
Reconstruct me now, trust His process, it's true

It wasn't until my total surrender was complete
I submitted my spirit, soul, and body, now I'm at
His feet
My entire reliance on God is now concrete

Never Fails

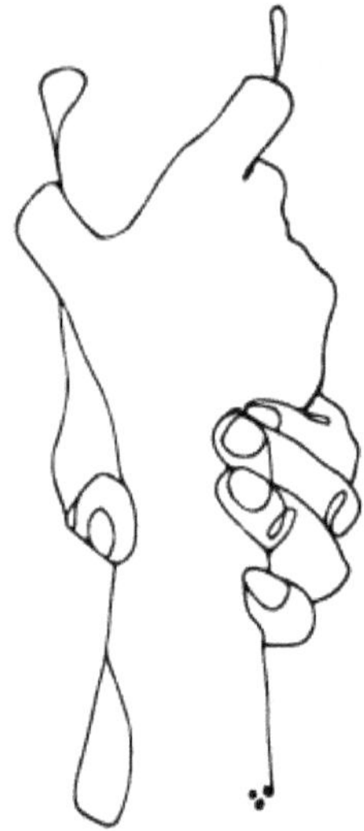

I used to have to see before I would believe
What You had in store for me I ignored

Things You led me to You wanted me to do
Naïve and unsure my faith was insecure

But now that I see You always know what's best
for me
And I choose to follow You, You always see me
through

You're the only one, that whenever I call You
are always there
Trusting in You never fails and You're the only
one, that whatever I need
You always provide following You never fail

Now that I see, You always know what's best for
me
And I choose to follow You, You always see me
through

You're the only one, that whenever I call You
are always there
Trusting in You never fails and You're the only
one, whatever I need
You always provide following you never fail

No matter what I'm going through
There's nothing too big for me to bring to You

You're the only one, You died for me
You give me victory and strength whenever I
need
I owe it all, I owe it all, I owe it all

Conqueror, Comforter, Provider, Savior, never
fails
My Conqueror, Comforter, Provider, Savior,
never fails

I owe it all, I owe it all, I owe it all, I owe it all,
never fails

Seasons Come and Seasons Go

There is a season and a time for every purpose
under heaven
Seasons come and seasons go without question

Seasons don't have to get permission to make a
change
When seasons change God doesn't even have to
explain

Adapting to seasons causes a change and shift
Accepting life's inevitable moments is like a gift

Seasons will prepare you and they might get
scary
Shifting loads of weight, you may have to carry

Sooner or later you'll realize life's seasons are
temporary
Accepting what God allows will make you
extraordinary

What Is Value?

Value, is it worth the amount of a dollar?
Does life's uncertainties equate to a holler?
Could it be surviving the perplexed pressures of
life?
Could it be celebrating victory after strife?

It's the fresh, gusty wind blowing
It's the Ruach of the Almighty all-knowing
Increasing our value is what life's about
If God places value on something we should
seek it out

Value, is it worth the amount of a quarter?

Is it me as sheep being accounted for slaughter?
Could it be about life's untimely interruptions?
Could it be life's many unannounced
reconstructions?

It's miraculously being able to distinctly see
It's the divine plan, the Creator, meticulously
crafted for me
His intentions the entire time; He always knew
His love for Me was unconditional; Breathe and
life into me He blew

Value, is it worth the amount of a dime?
Is it the heartbeat of life's rhythm and rhyme?
Could it be the cost of agonizing pain?
Could it be unforeseen losses with nothing to
gain?

It's the confession of love that He couldn't hide
It's the Agape Love He expressed as blood
trickled from His side
The cost of the cross would finish; the devil's
schemes He diminished
If belief bore the significance of the cross; the
Savior guaranteed we don't have to be lost

Value, is it worth the amount of a nickel or a
penny?

Is it deciphering what is real, fake, or artificial if
any?
Could it be that Jesus carved out a space for me
to be birthed?
Could it be that I've finally ascertained my
self-worth?

It's the shattered pieces of destiny and the
pursuit of a mission
It's the desires of my heart that bring Your will
into fruition
Billions and millions couldn't equate God's
worth
God's purpose for creation; establishing
relationships with Him on earth

A Backslider's Love

Never think when sin is present,
you'll live life to its fullest,
then get saved.
Tomorrow isn't promised
the devil will help you take
your treasures to your grave.

Never think you're not good enough
to give your life to Christ.
Jesus is waiting on you,
His life for you He sacrificed.

The world categorizes your sins
with their unforgivable way of thinking.
Jesus came to give life abundantly
with the realization, your sinful life is sinking.

Don't ever think you've sinned too much and in
you, He'll never dwell.
Ask Him to save your soul,
a lost sheep coming home He won't repel.

You think you're too messed up
and haven't served as a faith provider.
Listen carefully, He'll lovingly articulate

He's always married to the backslider.

So listen, backslider, don't stress,
let Jesus in your heart.
He'll forgive your sins and He'll give you a fresh
start!

Lord, You are so awesome
for giving me a second chance.
I'll forever learn to praise You
even in advance.

I tried to do the best I could.
Sometimes sin was ever present before me.
Even when I failed, you let me know
You were the key to my destiny.

Nothing to offer in this world but the lust of the
flesh, the lust of the eyes, and a life full of pride.
Lord, forgive me even now, I ask for
forgiveness, I desperately want to be your bride.

Help me not to miss heaven's opportunities to
gain temporal treasures, it's what this world is
about.
Right now Father, thank you for forgiving me,
fill me with your Holy Spirit and I'll never walk
in doubt.

Don't Be Afraid of Change

Change is needed when you've stopped believing
believing
Mountains appear humongous albeit misleading

Feeling stuck and closed in life brings
immobility
Confusion at an all-time high longing for
tranquility

Unrevealed, not knowing what's next, the
unknown

No more room for vision and imagination,
growth has outgrown

It's the place of unknown, I found God attaching
newness to me
Taught me how to live my life in complete
victory

Down on my knees talking to the Lord in prayer
He'll let you know, my child, I was always right
there

The problem wasn't the fact that my Jesus didn't
answer
It was the fear of change worrying me, eating
my mind like a cancer

Wisdom is asking God what do I do next to
embrace the change
Waiting on confirmation will help when the
Almighty begins to rearrange

Keeping me from lies, hurt, harm, and danger,
even now
Accept inevitable change and appreciate what
God will allow

Wait On the Lord

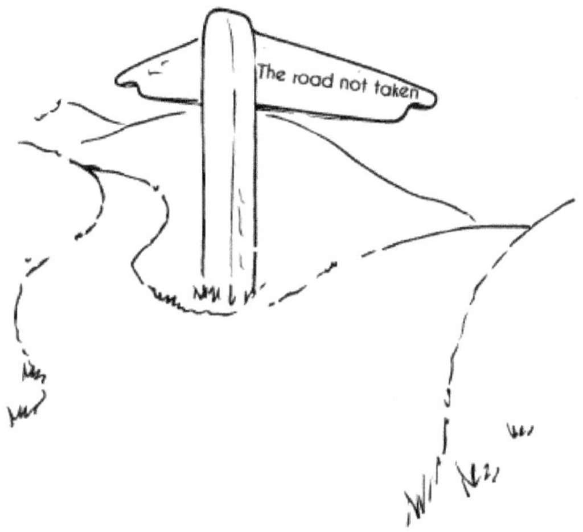

Wait on the Lord, you won't regret it
No need to worry, no need to sweat it

Yes, I know you got it all figured out
Waiting on the Lord is the shortest route

Don't take a journey designed for 11 days
Turn it into 40 years because you're stuck in
your ways

Waiting makes you a doer and not just a hearer

Acting in God's timing makes your vision much
clearer

Patience is the capacity to accept or tolerate
delay, without anger
Time is of the essence, weighing on my mind
like an anchor

Wait on the Lord, you'll be glad you did
Waiting on God's voice is being transparent not
hid

I know you've heard all of this before
Yield your all to him right now, He'll fill you
with so much more

Jealousy

God blessed me while pursuing my destiny
I witnessed the devil's, unpleasant doses of
jealousy

Talking about me behind my back
The maturity and bravery to confront you lack

Got a glimpse of the favor in my life
Wanted the favor but your jealousy increased
with strife

I didn't understand the depth of your jealousy
Until you gossiped and fabricated lies so
fearlessly

Sharing venomous opinions, your number one
distractor
The enemy, the accuser, my character you were
always after

Weren't your accomplishments enough to bring
you great joy
Guess not, since the enemy used you like his
little toy

The entire time I knew the fruits of the spirit
must be hid
Every time you opened your mouth, God heard
the evil you did

Eyes are always focused on us, the children of
God
Welcoming the darkness, fulfilling your purpose
trying to make life hard

The enemy never gives the details in the line he
uses, you see
God communicated to the spirit of jealousy how
He'll protect me

I'm still standing to tell the story while walking
in His Glory
In the Book of Life, God will judge us by
checking inventory

I pray your jealousy, hatred, and envy have
diminished over the years
Jesus Christ still saves, run to Him before He
returns and salvation disappears

Revelation 22:11 says, "He that is filthy and
unjust, let him be filthy and unjust still"
God loves you enough He'll never force you to
do anything against your own free will

Spiritual Vision

You couldn't see the hand, God had on me
You plotted anyhow and you did it for free

You couldn't recognize the shining light above
my head
Oh, I guess you chose darkness over light
instead

You couldn't see your actions as diminishing
words as sin
God's discernment reveals actions and words
from within

You didn't see me pondering and crying out to
God, asking "Why?"
It didn't matter, you accepted sin willfully and
chose to die

You couldn't see yourself walking around as a
dead corpse
Carrying out the will of the devil you
professionally support

You couldn't see the satanic vessel you had
become
Comprehending the spiritual realm you were far
from

You couldn't see you were walking in a form of
ungodliness

God's love can provide you with an aroma of
holiness

You couldn't see the scales covering your eyes
So busy representing satan in your carnal
disguise

Have you acknowledged your wrong and
decided to repent
God is still calling you, double-minded people is
why He was sent

The enemy doesn't care who he uses, your
decision
Open your eyes, let Jesus be your spiritual vision

No Need to Wonder

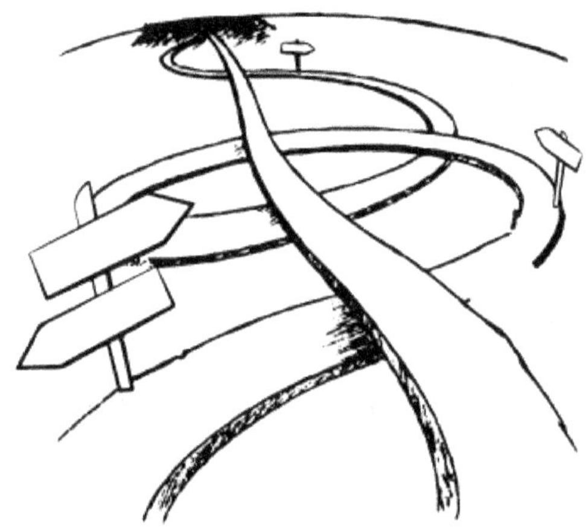

I've always wondered why I had trouble fitting
in
Was it because of my appearance and
personality, where should I begin

I've always wondered why the subtle light jokes
My child-like heart you unconsciously broke

I've always wondered why things seem to go so
wrong

Did I not hear or listen to God or maybe
pondered too long

I've always wondered why life kept repeating
itself over
Was it because God protected and then He'd get
exposure

I've always wondered why friends silently
walked away
God answered my wonder and said, "They were
never meant to stay"

I've always wondered why I was chosen for
life's harsh tests
God conveyed to me they were distinctly
designed for your best

I've always wondered if I was the only one
being tested
God responded, "No, everyone who seeks me, in
them, I've invested"

I've always wondered when the tests finally
would subside, what next
Tests are a part of the plan, you're My chosen
elect.
No more wondering

Love At Its Best

It was love that broke my heart
I would have reconsidered had I known from the
start

How could I not want to become full of love
When my own Creator Himself sent love from
up above

You see, unconditional love always lurks around
Waiting to be noticed, waiting to be found

It was love that lifted me
And placed me right where I needed to be

When love is at its best it never really walks
away
Love at its worst? It's imitational and never
really intends to stay

My heart, my mind, and my spirit are free
Free to love without discriminating in the least

Keep It Real

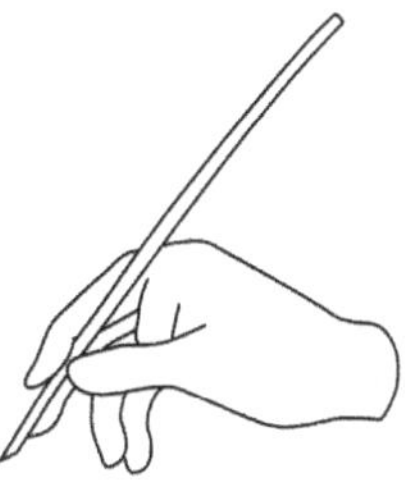

Let's keep it real, I've had some good days and some bad
Being able to get back up has been the best time I've ever had

Learning to replace sorrow with laughter and joy
Knowing my life the enemy was not allowed to destroy

Let's keep it real when it looks like all hope is gone
Have no fear, joy, unspeakable joy comes at dawn

Confronting life's most difficult moments is true
Tell him your heart's desire and make it happen for you

Let's keep it real, life happened right before my
eyes
When I was real with Him, He answered all of
my cries

The best relationship I ever could have
developed in life
Was the communication and relationship I've
had with Jesus, the Christ

Let's keep it real, He never goes back on His
Word
He has extraordinary Power, haven't you heard

If you still have, that voided place in your heart
I caution you right now, Jesus is the best place to
start

Just keeping it real